NIGHTMARE CREATURES

SPIDERS!

BLACK WIDOW SPIDERS

Joanne Randolph

PowerKiDS
press.

New York

Published in 2014 by The Rosen Publishing Group, Inc.
29 East 21st Street, New York, NY 10010

First Edition

Editor: Jennifer Way and Norman D. Graubart
Book Design: Andrew Povolny
Photo Research: Katie Stryker

Photo Credits: Cover, p. 17 (top) Kallista Images/Getty Images; p. 4 iStockphoto/Thinkstock; p. 5 Brian Chase/Shutterstock.com; p. 6 Peter Waters/Shutterstock.com; p. 7 (top)Colton Stiffler/Shutterstock.com; p. 7 (bottom) Hemera Technologies/Photos.com/Thinkstock; p. 9 DSTU/Shutterstock.com; p. 10 © iStockphoto/Pete Pattavina; p. 11 E R Degginger/Photo Researchers/Getty Images; pp. 12–13 © iStockphotos/Keith Szafranski; p. 14, 18 H Robinson James/Photo Researchers/Getty Images; p. 15 Les Stocker/Oxford Scientific/Getty Images; p. 16 Hway Kiong Lim/Shutterstock.com; p. 17 (bottom) © iStockphoto/ArmanDavtyan p. 19 Natures Images/Photo Researchers/Getty Images; p. 21 Elliotte Rusty Harold/Shutterstock.com; p. 22 Jessica Lewis/Flickr/Getty Images.

Library of Congress Cataloging-in-Publication Data

Randolph, Joanne, author.
 Black widow spiders / by Joanne Randolph. — First edition.
     pages cm. — (Nightmare creatures. Spiders!)
 Includes index.
 ISBN 978-1-4777-2888-8 (library) — ISBN 978-1-4777-2977-9 (pbk.) —
ISBN 978-1-4777-3047-8 (6-pack)
 1. Black widow spider—Juvenile literature. I. Title.
 QL458.42.T54R36 2014
 595.4'4—dc23
                              2013021647

Manufactured in the United States of America

CPSIA Compliance Information: Batch #W14PK6: For Further Information contact Rosen Publishing, New York, New York at 1-800-237-9932

CONTENTS

MEET THE BLACK WIDOW SPIDER

Imagine an animal with **venom** that is 13 times more powerful than a rattlesnake's venom. Imagine that the female animals eat the males of the **species**. That sounds like a horrible creature that lives in nightmares. You have just met the black widow spider.

Like most spiders, black widows make webs. This female black widow is weaving her web.

This red, hourglass-like marking on the abdomen is common to the black widow spider.

This 1.5-inch (3.8 cm) spider is part of a group of animals called arachnids. Black widows have glossy black bodies and round **abdomens**. Males tend to be smaller, with longer, narrower abdomens. All black widow spiders belong to a **genus** called *Latrodectus*.

Black widow spiders can be found on every continent on Earth except Antarctica. There are 32 species in the genus. The spiders in the family they are part of are commonly called tangle-web spiders. They get this name because they weave messy, tangled webs out of their sticky silk.

This female Australian redback spider, a member of the black widow family, is dangling in the middle of her web waiting to catch prey.

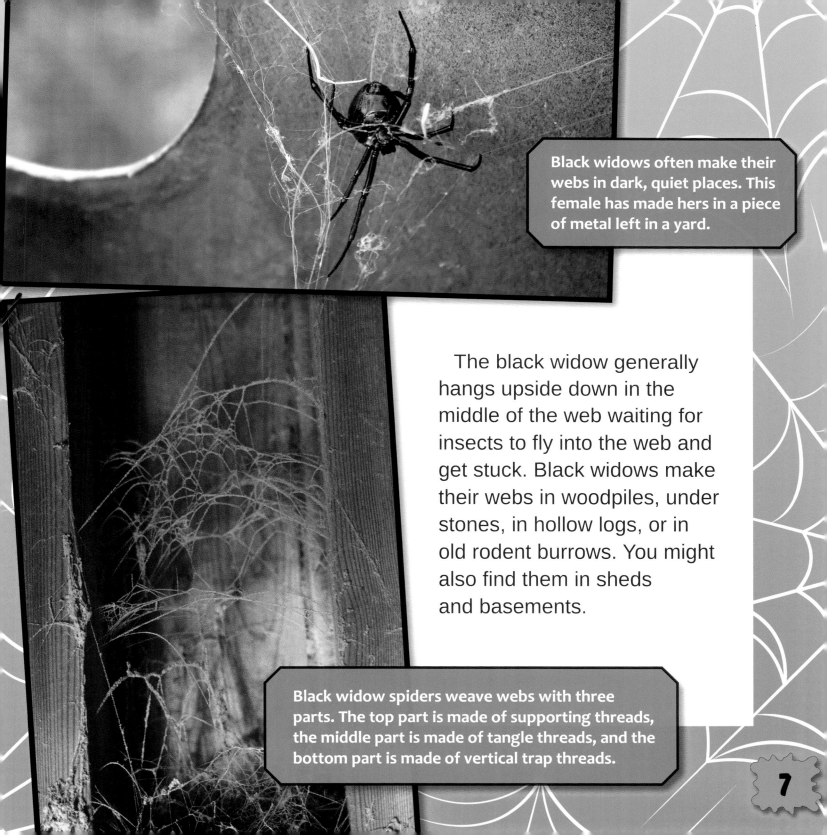

Black widows often make their webs in dark, quiet places. This female has made hers in a piece of metal left in a yard.

The black widow generally hangs upside down in the middle of the web waiting for insects to fly into the web and get stuck. Black widows make their webs in woodpiles, under stones, in hollow logs, or in old rodent burrows. You might also find them in sheds and basements.

Black widow spiders weave webs with three parts. The top part is made of supporting threads, the middle part is made of tangle threads, and the bottom part is made of vertical trap threads.

ARACHNIDS

Black widows are arachnids. Like all arachnids, they have two body parts. These two parts are the head and the abdomen. They have eight legs and two parts that look like two extra sets of legs. One of these parts is the mouth. The other extra parts are called the **pedipalps**. These can be used for feeding, moving, or reproduction, depending on the species.

Black widow spiders are black with red markings on the undersides of their abdomens. The red markings often look like an hourglass, but they can also look like two red dots. Males are smaller and duller in color. They generally have red and white stripes on the sides of their bodies.

You can clearly see the pedipalps on this black widow. They are the two appendages that point inward at the very middle of the spider's head.

VENOM!

Black widow spiders bite their **prey** to kill them. They use powerful venom to help **paralyze** their prey. When they bite insects, they also put matter into their bodies that makes everything inside the body become **liquid**. They then suck up the liquid.

Black widows are not very big, but a tiny bite can cause pain and discomfort, even for a human.

This black widow is biting a caterpillar. After only a few minutes of muscle spasms, the caterpillar will become paralyzed and die.

When a black widow spider bites a human, the human's insides do not become liquid. However, the venom in the black widow's bite causes horrible muscle pain and even makes it so the person cannot move his body parts. Most of the time, the pain goes away in a few days and the person does not die. Sometimes, children, older people, or people who are sick can be killed by a black widow spider bite.

NIGHTMARE FACTS

1. Black widow spiders are the most venomous spiders in North America. Most people will not die from a bite, though.

2. The tips of the black widow spider's legs are coated in oil. This keeps the spider from sticking to the sticky strands of the web.

3. Black widow females lay around 200 eggs at a time. They wrap their eggs in pear-shaped sacs made of silk.

4. The baby spiders may stay in their cocoon for 30 days after hatching before they come out and leave the web.

5. Black widow spiders are nocturnal. They hide in special retreats made from silk during the day. At night, the female comes out and hangs in the center of the web.

6. Their silk is very strong. During World War II, black widow spider silk was used to make crosshairs for American guns.

SOLITARY SPIDERS

Black widow spiders spend most of their time alone. They hang in their webs without moving for long periods of time. They spend time with other spiders only when it is time to mate.

The brown widow spider is very similar to the black widow. It is less poisonous, but its red marking is similar to the black widow's. This is called mimicking.

14

Steatodas **are also called false widow spiders. Do you see any similarities between** *steatodas* **and black widow spiders?**

Not much is known about whether spiders communicate with one another. However, the black widow's red markings are there to send a clear message to the animal world. That message is, "I am poisonous. Leave me alone!" Many animals that have venom **glands** also carry these warning colors. *Steatoda* spiders look very similar to black widows but lack the red markings on their abdomens. Their bites are far less harmful than black widows', even though they look almost the same.

WHAT'S FOR DINNER?

Black widow spiders are **insectivores**. This means they eat mainly insects, such as flies, grasshoppers, beetles, and caterpillars. If an insect lands in its web, the spider springs into action. It will hurry through its web to the prey.

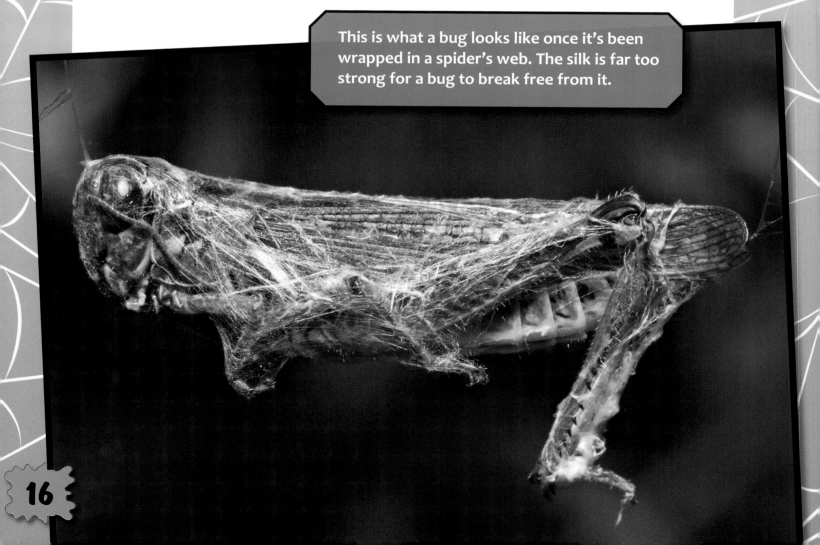

This is what a bug looks like once it's been wrapped in a spider's web. The silk is far too strong for a bug to break free from it.

This close-up image shows the hairy bristles on the spider's legs. These bristles make it easier for the black widow to wrap its prey in silk.

Black widow spiders are part of a group of spiders sometimes called comb-footed spiders. This is because they have sets of bristles, or hairs, on their back legs. They use these bristles to wrap their prey in silk. The black widow then bites its prey. Its venom turns the insides of the bug to liquid.

This black widow spider is waiting for an insect to land in its web. If the black widow spider does not quickly wrap the insect in its silk, then the insect could get away.

BABY BLACK WIDOWS

When a male black widow is ready to mate, he leaves his web to search for a female. This can take some time. Once he has found one, he vibrates her web in a special way to make sure she is the right species and to let her know he is there to mate. Once she recognizes that the male spider is not prey, they can mate. Sometimes the female will eat the male once mating has occurred!

This male black widow is courting a female. Spiders have poor eyesight, so she has to feel the vibrations of the web to learn that the creature is not an enemy, but a mate.

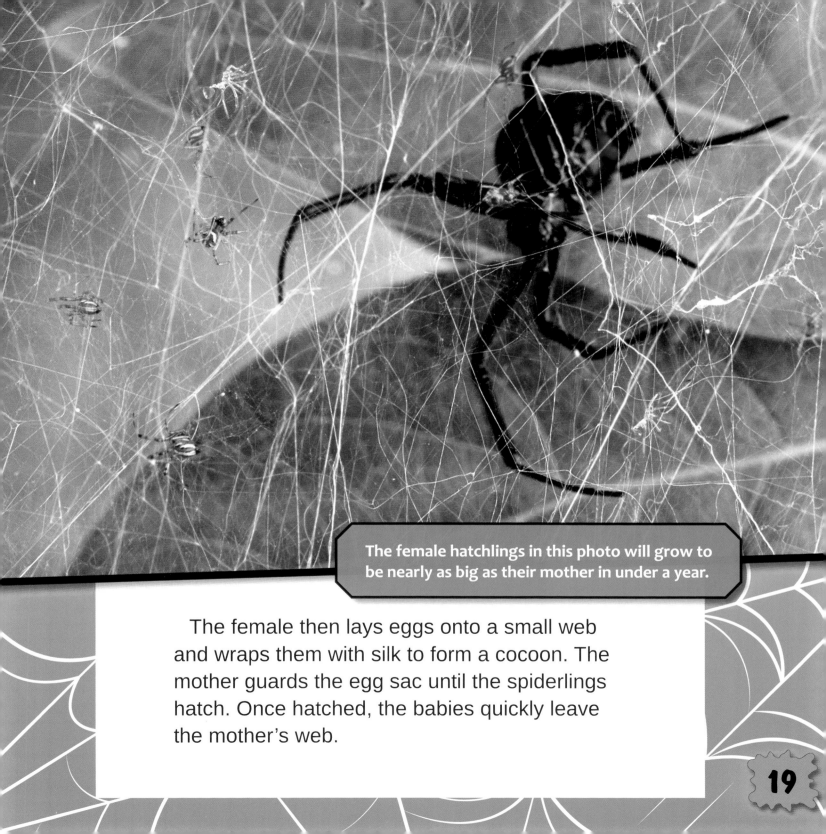

The female hatchlings in this photo will grow to be nearly as big as their mother in under a year.

The female then lays eggs onto a small web and wraps them with silk to form a cocoon. The mother guards the egg sac until the spiderlings hatch. Once hatched, the babies quickly leave the mother's web.

DON'T EAT ME!

The black widow spider does not have many known **predators**. Its web serves as a good defense against most insect predators. However, the mud-dauber wasp has been known to get past this sticky defense and make a meal of the black widow.

The black widow's red markings are another defense. They tell would-be predators, such as birds, that making a meal out of this spider would be a bad idea.

If a larger animal or a person disturbs its web, the black widow spider may drop from its web and pretend to be dead. If a person sits on the spider, it may bite in self-defense.

Mud-dauber wasps also have venom that paralyzes their prey. If a mud-dauber can get past a black widow's web, it can give the black widow a taste of its own medicine!

Many people fear black widows because of their venomous bite. It is true that a bite from a black widow can be quite painful and needs medical attention. Despite what people think, though, the bite is rarely deadly.

People also need to remember that black widows are not lurking in the dark, hoping people will come by so they can bite them. The black widow's first reaction would be to hide or play dead. It bites people only if it thinks it is in danger. If we treat black widow spiders with respect and do not bother them in their webs, they are more than happy to leave us alone, too.

While medical treatment can help you if you are bitten by a black widow, it is always best to keep some distance between yourself and a black widow spider.

GLOSSARY

abdomens (AB-duh-munz) The large, rear parts of insects' bodies.

genus (JEE-nus) The scientific name for a group of plants or animals that are alike.

glands (GLANDZ) Organs or parts of the body that produce elements to help with bodily functions.

insectivores (in-SEK-tih-vorz) Animals that eat insects for food.

liquid (LIH-kwed) Matter that flows.

paralyze (PER-uh-lyz) To cause loss of feeling or movement.

pedipalps (PEH-duh-palps) Appendages on arachnids.

predators (PREH-duh-terz) Animals that kill other animals for food.

prey (PRAY) An animal that is hunted by another animal for food.

species (SPEE-sheez) One kind of living thing. All people are one species.

venom (VEH-num) A poison passed by one animal into another through a bite or a sting.

INDEX

WEBSITES